Copywriting

A Beginner's Blueprint

How To Write Amazing Copy
That Compels Readers To Take
Action Without Selling Your Soul

By Adam Richards

Table of Contents

Introduction

Writing, be it books, stories, or blogs, is a fulfilling endeavor. What this means is that any form of writing does require some passion for writing. Earlier on in the development of writing as a profession, writers had limited options. They had only two options: write a book, or write a play. With technological advancements and an ever-changing world, writing has evolved into something that the world appreciates, loves, and turns to for advice, inspiration, and direction on a specific subject.

Writing as a subject has evolved and branched out into various categories. Today, writers have a plethora of writing fields they can choose to pursue. One of these fields is copyrighting.

If this is your first brush with copywriting, you are probably wondering what it is. Not to worry, I will give you an in-depth look of exactly what copywriting is, and how you can become great at it.

Chapter 1:

Copywriting 101

Understanding The Concept Of Copywriting

What exactly is copywriting? Make a guess. Now, with your guess still fresh in your mind, let me give you a true glimpse of what copywriting is.

Copywriting is the aspect of writing copies for the sole purpose of marketing or advertising. The written copy is a piece of document meant to persuade a potential buyer or customer to buy the product, or influence how they view the product in question differently.

In broadcasting, marketing, and advertising, someone who writes copies is called a copywriter or continuity (in broadcasting). The work of a copywriter is straightforward: create taglines, webpage content, and direct mail pieces. Copywriters who write web content prefer the name content writer to copywriters.

The scope of responsibilities a copywriter holds in his or her cap is not limited to the above list; it goes further than that. Copywriters also create newsletters, online ads, internet content, press releases, catalogs, brochures, and other marketing materials, TV and radio commercial scripts and many more.

Additionally, a copywriter also has some role to play in book publishing. In this field, the copywriter is responsible for writing the jacket flap and flap copy with a compelling summary of the book. As I have indicated, technology space has expanded tremendously. Today, copywriters are also very prevalent in social media, social networking, and blog posts.

Before the advent of technology, and the freelancing craze, copywriters were (and still are), employees within organizations such as public relation firms, advertising agencies, book publishers, creative agencies, and advertising departments within organizations. This has changed to a certain degree with the rise of the internet.

Many copywriters are choosing to become independent. They are choosing to freelance for different clients and specialized copywriting agencies. In this type of setting, the copywriter has more 'string' to his or her writing because they are able to perform tasks such as editing, message consulting, SEO consulting, proofreading, design and layout etc.

As a copywriter, you will have to be a team player because often, copywriters work within the confines of a creative team. For example, if you work for an advertising agency, the organization may pair you with an art director. However, your main role is to create a verbally and textually compelling content derived from the copy provided by the client. In essence, the responsibility of a copywriter is to tell a story; a story that resonates with the reader, viewer, or potential customer.

I find it necessary to point out that there is little difference between a copywriter and a technical writer. The only difference between the two is that the work of a technical writer is simply to inform and not persuade. Here is a good comparison of the two parts of writing despite the fact that the careers of either often overlap. A content writer's work is to write a car ad to persuade a potential customer, while the work of a technical writer is to write about the operations of the car from reading the manual.

If you are wondering why you should bother learning the skill of copywriting, here are a few reasons.

\# As a copywriter, you get a chance to influence the masses by creating an ad or creative piece that remains on the mind of the viewer.

\# You get to work in the exciting field of advertising for TV and radio. In addition, you get to interact with some interesting people in the field of broadcasting.

\# Content writing is a creative venture. Therefore, if you love writing, you get to enjoy yourself while making a ton of money (yes, copywriting is a very profitable business concept).

Now that you have a better understanding of what copywriting is, let us look at five things every copywriter should know.

8

Chapter 2:

What Every Beginner

Copywriter Needs To Know

Creating compelling copies demands a sort of inside information to what moves the masses or what builds up emotions in the specific target viewer or buyer. As we saw in the previous chapter, the work of a copywriter is to tell a story. To create compelling copies, you need to know your characters to get a story that compels them. This is the first principle of copywriting.

To create copies that grip the attention of your reader, you need to understand who they are and know them intimately. Fortunately, I have some tips to help you do exactly that. Here are five very important things every copywriter should bear in mind.

One: Your 'target' reader or target wants to feel important

The number one desire that motivates any 'target' is importance. This is the most basic concept of copywriting you must accept and adapt. Let us look at this concept in-depth. Did you know that the minutest of actions are all in our attempts for importance in the world? Think about it for a minute. The way you dress, walk, and talk is meant to curve your space in the world. Most of the actions of creating an importance about us stems from our goals to be something or someone in society. The same applies to creating compelling copies. To resonate with the masses or an audience, a copy must make them feel important.

A company can create this importance by creating better content or layout on their website to create the feeling of importance to visiting clients. The concept is simple. Better content layout or tools keep the customer coming back repeatedly. If you can glimpse what makes the customer feel important, you can then use this information to stir some emotion in them and influence them into buying a product or liking a post.

Two: Most 'targets' are insecure

(In the above title, 'target' stands for the audience or buyer).

It is a fact that no one on the face of the earth is totally content with whom or what he or she is. This is true even for the rich and powerful. If everyone were content, and happy, we would never have the need to do anything. Most of us are insecure. Insecurities cause dissatisfaction. This dissatisfaction then causes us to pursue endeavors and activities aimed at creating some sense of importance. Copywriting, depending on the target must play on these insecurities to influence the target.

A good example of the difference in insecurities is the motivation to stay fit or lose weight. Each person who decides to embark on this has different motivation. Here is something you should consider. If you were to create a copy for a weight loss product, you would need to account for the difference in motivation. For example, the copy for someone (let's say a guy) who is embarrassed about their body would be different from another person whose motivation to get fit is chronic ailment. This means that you can use the 'insecurities' and motivation of the target to create copies that speak to their emotions.

This is especially true when the same fitness product may suit both. The approach to marketing the product to these classes of people will vary greatly. This means, to create a copy for either of the target groups, the message on the copy has to resonate at a deep level with the customers by addressing their goals and tackling their fears.

Three: Glimpsing into their past can give you clues and help you create better copies

By looking at the vital clues in the target past, you can create better copies. Most marketers target the customer as they are today. However, the past is also important in creating outstanding copies. By looking into their past, you can get a glimpse of what they have been through, the problems they face today, and the emotions that are likely to influence their purchases. Remember that we have already understood that to create awesome copies, you must understand their character. This means that you have to go back into their past and look at the factors that made them who they are.

To compound this, think of it from the mindset of your customer. Most of the purchases we make are emotional in nature. The emotion could be convenience or anything else. The fact is that it is still an emotion. This means that to create a compelling copy, you have to get into the mind of the customer and unravel the events and mysteries of why they are the way they are.

For example, if you are writing a copy for a small business owner, you have to understand how they got to where they are, what made them want to go into business? How long have they been in business? Think of it in terms of writing a memoir. To write one, you must get the story from the horse's mouth, so to say.

The same applies to creating copies. Going through the motions of the targets' past gives you a better view of their desire, and helps you create better, appealing copies. Checking the targets' past may seem intrusive, but it is not. It is the make or break factor that helps you shape content and themes around the desires and appeal of the target customer.

Here is a sneak preview of some of the basic pasts of a business owner, try to write copies for each.

A business owner forced into business due to the impact of the recession.

A person who goes into business after college.

How would the copies you create for these groups vary?

Four: Conflict is the window into the true character of the target

During periods of conflict, a person's true character shines through. Creating 'killer' copies demands an understanding of your targets' conflict. While some conflicts are as simple as an action that causes some problem and a solution for that problem (for example, if your car breaks down when you need to be somewhere, the most logical option is to call AA or a mechanic), some conflicts are not subtle. For example, a business owner who wants a polished website to create an air of importance to the viewer presents no real conflict.

However, if you dig, deeper, you may find that the business worries about their professional appearance. This does not create a conflict. If you dig even deeper, you may find that the business owner may have insecurities if they are new to the market, does not have a clue on how to create a website, and must hire someone to do the designing. This is a conflict. The firm or individual who understands and appreciates this conflict can then create content for that specific client better than a company can or individual that ambiguously offers website development.

I should also point out that knowing a person's individual story is not important. What is important is to know the conflict they face. This is especially for categories of individuals and businesses in the same field that have similar conflicts. With this, you can then write a copy that appeals to them.

Five: How far are they willing to go?

Fictionally, you need to gauge how far your target is willing to go. Is he or she willing to go bankrupt? Commit a crime, or embark on an adventure to achieve their dream? To create outstanding copies, you must know how far the customer is willing to go. It is not necessary to know where they are willing to go for the solution. What is important is to what length they would go to resolve a conflict.

This includes the price they are willing to pay; is it an impulse buy, or are they willing to shop around? How keen are they to solve the conflict? You may also need to know how quickly they want to solve the conflict, and to what extent they are willing to work with you or otherwise on the conflict.

With the above, you can then commence on researching what makes them tick and use this to try new approaches, and ways to present a solution to the conflict. For example, if you are writing a copy for a product, and know that the customer is willing to shop around, you can compare the content in question to other content or create content for this.

More importantly, you should note that understanding the target client is not moonwalk. It is hard and takes time: it is not instant coffee. This is the sole purpose why the creative team within which a copywriter works can spend many hours brainstorming, creating ideas and approaches, dismissing them, and creating others.

Now that we understand the concept of creating a copy from the perspective of the target market, let us move on swiftly. In the next chapter, we shall look at some common mistakes beginner copywriters make, and how you can avoid them.

Chapter 3:

The 7 Most Common Mistakes Made By Inexperienced Copywriters - And How To Avoid Them

While making mistakes is acceptable, making mistakes in copywriting can mean a million or zero sales or hits. If copies are not effective, they are no better than an inadequate marketing campaign. You must understand the whole point of copywriting is to drum up sales. Therefore, if a copy does not achieve this, it is ineffective.

Many beginner copywriters are especially prone to making mistakes that hinder the effectiveness of the copy. There is no reason you should also make the same mistakes. To make sure you do not follow the mistake-ridden path that most copywriters make, let us look at some of the common mistakes they make.

Mistake One: Boring and drab headlines

Did you know that about 80% of people would click through to an article only if the tittle is compelling? If the tittle of an article or the tagline of a product does not compel the reader, there is little chance that this will translate into sales. Think about it. What would interest you more, a headline that reads 'our membership plan', or one that reads, 'Ten reasons you should choose our membership plan?' Which of the two do you think would be most effective? In most cases, and to most customers, the latter of the two would be more interesting and compelling. If your copywriting endeavor is to be successful, you cannot make this fatal mistake.

To create compelling headlines and avoid this mistake, ask yourself this one question. What is it that the person reading this is looking for? What do they want? If you can answer this question, it is easier to create headlines that stir some emotion in the reader.

Mistake Two: Underwhelming content

You have created a killer headline. The next step is to make the contents of the copy just as compelling as the headline. I see this mistake a lot. Copywriters create awesome headlines, but create less-then-stellar content. What you should know is that the headline grabs the attention of the reader, but the content makes them stay and or decide to buy.

The best way to avoid this is by using the methods we described in the previous chapter. You need to get into the head of the target and discover what they want to hear. What makes them important? You can then use this information to create super awesome content for your copy. Furthermore, I have to point out that the content should not be too short or too long. If it is too short, it will leave the reader wondering what next. If it is too long, it will bore the reader to death. Your work then becomes striking a balance between the two.

Mistake Three: Focusing primarily on the product features

While this may seem like a logical approach, it is in fact wrong. The customer does not really care about the product features. What they want to know is how it benefits them or how does it solve their conflict? Most new copywriters make the mistake of failing to vividly highlight the benefits of the product and simply focus on the features. Do not let this be you.

Focus on the features, let them take a back seat. Start your copy by highlighting the various benefits of using the product and then finish the copy off with the product features.

Mistake four: Creating copies that the customer cannot relate to

Sometimes, even the most experienced copywriters make this mistake. Good copies must take into account the reader, customer, or potential buyer. The reader must relate with the content on an emotional level for the copy to be effective.

You can avoid this mistake by doing research on the target or framing your copy in words that relate to them. For example, when writing a copy to market weight-loss products, you need to create content and use words that relate to a weight loss enthusiast.

Mistake Five: Writing copies that do not invoke an emotional response

An emotional response is something I would consider a critical principle to creating good copies. Good copies instill a sense of emotional response from the reader or buyer. The copy must motivate the reader into some form of action. It (the copy) must have the right tone in respect to the target market or consumer. If a copy falls short of creating an emotional connection with the consumer, it is a flop.

Avoiding this mistake is relatively easy. All you need to do is frame your content in the mind frame of the target.

Mistake Six: Content that is not visually appealing and has a poor layout

Your content and its layout must be visually appealing. If you work as a copywriter in an advertising agency, the company will pair you with a creative director. However, if you are creating content for a website, you can make the content appealing by integrating images. Further, you can achieve a fluid layout by breaking down the content into bite size chunks that are easy to read.

A good way to eliminate this mistake is by using

headings and bullet points, paragraph headers, short paragraphs and sentences, and product screenshots.

Mistake Seven: Failure to integrate a call to action

A call to action could be anything. It could be a call to sign-up, asking the target to do something, or take some form of action. A call to action is indeed what it is: a call to take action. This is a 'wild-fire' mistake that many copywriters make unknowingly. After creating a killer headline and well-thought out content that connects with the reader, the next logical step is to ask them to take some action on the content they have read. A call to action is the final piece in asking the consumer to buy the product. Like the headlines, the call to action must be compelling and interesting. Where you place the call to action is also important.

A clever way to avoid this mistake is offer pointed content and create a call to action that shows the benefits of the product. The call to action should be subtle. If you are creating copies for a website, you can integrate colorful call to action buttons. Some popular call to action buttons and texts are:

Get instant access!

Get free access!

Get started now!

Chapter 4:

Copywriting Basics: The ABC's Of Writing Compelling Copy

Copywriters use a wide array of tools in their toolbox to create compelling content. One area that is often overlooked by many copywriters is creating content. Whether you are a literature major or the average Joe who loves writing, or a complete beginner starting out in copywriting, the skills you need to create compelling copies are similar. You must enrich your editorial and writing skills.

As we have already seen, a good copy helps the reader or buyer understand the offer and how it benefits them (what we called solving a conflict). You can use a thousand and one tips and strategies to create compelling copies. All of them may be effective. Here are some of the ABC's of writing compelling copy. Adhering to these (let's call them commandments) will help you create compelling copies each time.

First Commandment: Know and understand your target

In an earlier chapter, we talked about 'getting into the mind of the audience'. This is critical in writing good copies. When writing a copy, visualize the intended audience. Bring your characters into life. Then, think of what would make them feel important, what problems and conflicts they are going through, how old they are, and the type of products that interest them. More information about the target audience means better understanding and translates into better and targeted copies.

Second Commandment: Know the value of your product

After getting into the mind of the target, you then must consider the benefits this product adds to their life. You must have answers to questions such as why should the consumer buy the product, and how is your product better than other products. This will not only help you write better copies, it will also help you understand the client, which as we have seen is the best roadmap to writing compelling copies.

Third Commandment: Find a unique marketing angle

Advertisers spend hours, dollars, and workforce trying to outdo each other. Why do you think is the reason for this? Because when you stand out from the crowd, you tower above your competitors and other products. Furthermore, by finding a clever marketing angle and copy, you have a better chance of getting a response. A unique selling angle refers to a promotion plan or offer that is different from what the competition is offering. The uniqueness must also be compelling to drive product sales and attract customers.

Fourth Commandment: Be objective

Objectify your copy. What do I mean by this? I mean that you must define a purpose for the copy. Remember the call to action advice; this is the best way to objectify your copy. Objectifying your copy means that you have a clear goal of what you want the customer to do. Even before you start writing your copy, you must clearly define an objective. If the objective is not clear, you can bet that the copy will not be compelling to the reader.

Fifth commandment: Use a compelling headline or subject line

Earlier on, we looked at the importance of creating compelling headlines. A compelling headline is akin to a luminous blinking neon light. A headline is the first thing the reader sees. Therefore, it has to pull them in and make them want to read the content within the copy. What this means is that you have to spend a substantial amount of time creating a headline that is compelling even before you decide to write the copy.

When creating headlines, the most powerful word at your disposal is 'you'. You send a message that the content is all about them. Some other words you can use for your headlines are exclusive, new, exciting etc; any words that make the reader want to open or read the content. Additionally, you should aim to have a copy headline that is 50 characters or less.

Chapter 5:

Five Copywriting Rules That Can Make Or Break Your Copy

Thus far, we have dealt a lot with writing compelling copies and the mistakes you must avoid. You might also be wondering if there are any rules to writing copies; rules that can either make or break the effectiveness of your copy. Yes, there are some copywriting rules you should never break. If you break any of the following rules, your copy and ad is bound to be a total failure.

Before I list the rules, I have to point out that creating a bad copy is a recipe for product failure. Does this sound ambiguous? The reasoning behind this is simple. A bad copy hinders the rate of return on investment (ROI). It is as simple as that. This means that by creating a bad copy, you are unwittingly spelling failure to the product.

As we have seen, compelling copies must resonate with the target audience. This means that by failing to create, emotional, meaningful, and actionable copies, you are dooming the product before launch.

If you adhere to the following copyrighting rules, you are spelling success for the product and increasing your ROI.

Rule No1: Your product is far less important than the needs of the customer

How unique, advanced, or awesome your product is, is irrelevant if it does not solve the consumer's conflict. This means that instead of focusing on the product features, your focus should be its benefit to the user. It also means that what you feel or think about the product is irrelevant. What is relevant is what the product will make the consumer feel. What your consumer thinks about the product supersedes everything. It also means that by creating a copy that does not communicate an effective and emotional message, your product will definitely not be a success.

Rule No2: The 80-20 rule

Your copy should also follow the rule of the few. Therefore 80% of your copy should be in the second person voice. The second person is usage of the word 'you'. 20% or less should then be in the first person voice i.e. we or I. In copy, the consumer does not care about you; they care about what the products bring to their table. When creating a copy, you must answer the omnipresent consumer question "what's in it for me?" Answer this question by telling the consumer what they gain by purchasing the product.

Rule No3: The K.I.S.S. rule

KISS stands for 'keep it stupid simple'. Showing off your vocabulary in a copy is confusing to the audience. Therefore, save the big words for your creative writing. Choose your words as a master wine taster chooses his or her wine. If you are creating a copy for a car, use words that a car enthusiast would relate to and if you aim to create a copy for a weight loss product, use words that appeal to a weight loss enthusiast. Additionally, avoid using filler words such as very, really, and that as they only make your copy longer and hinder your message delivery.

Rule No4: The red pen rule

After completing your final copy, read it again and eliminate at least 30% of it. The red pen rule ensures the simplicity of your copy and helps you avoid overloading the consumer with too much information. Using the red pen rule also makes your message compact, succinct, and actionable.

Rule No5: The S.L.A.P. rule

SLAP is an acronym for a compelling copy that causes the consumer to:

Stop
Listen or Look
Act and
Purchase

This is similar to the call to action we looked at earlier. When writing a copy, do not leave the call to action as a suggestion. Demand some action from the consumer by using compelling content and words. Figuratively speaking, your copy should slap the target into action.

Chapter 6:

Copywriting Ethics: Staying True To Your Values

We have covered quite a lot about copywriting so far. By now, and if you have followed everything we have looked at, you should become at least a good copywriter. However, what about instances where you want to get better. What do you do then? Like many other professions, copywriting has some ethical rules meant to make you a better, happier, and content copywriter. Becoming a successful and happy copywriter, whether as a freelancer or within an organization, is indeed hard work.

Often, many freelance copywriters set unrealistic goals. This then creates tremendous stress on the individual. To be a success at copywriting, only one simple rule applies: success at work follows happiness.

If you are familiar with the law of attraction, you know what it states: we attract what we project. If you project positivity, you will be more successful in copywriting and other pillars of your life. You will also be productive, motivated, energetic, and resilient. To add to this, you must adopt an ethical approach to copywriting.

You can use the surprise and delight strategy to stay true to your values and be a happier copywriter.

What then is the surprise and delight strategy? The surprise and delight strategy states the following:

Define your success

If you are to achieve copywriting success, you must state what the success looks and feels like to you. Nobody will tell you or define for you a measure of your success. Rather than try to follow strategies from the so-called gurus, concentrate on defining your goals and success indicators.

Defining your success is the cornerstone to achieving them. Some pertinent questions you can use to define your success are:

How much money per month, do you want to make from copywriting?

How much free time do you require?

How many hours per day, will you work?

Which field of copywriting excites you?

Do you love telling stories or writing technically?

Not defining your goals and success measure will create a sense of instability. However, with defined success measures, once you achieve a goal, you can set a more ambitious one. Moreover, failing to define your goals and measure of success will hinder your insight: you will not be able to know when you achieve the goals or success. Create happiness and stability by defining what you aim to get from copywriting.

Pursue and aim to achieve the clients and consumer expectations

Most of what you will do as a copywriter is please others. On one end, you will struggle to please your boss (clients who hire you), and on the other end, please the consumer with compelling copies. From the client's side, secure a brief of the project. After reading the brief, explain to the client what they can expect from you.

Make sure that the expectation you project is one you can deliver.

In addition, since most clients are not copywriters (the whole reason behind hiring you) the briefs will have some deficiencies. Work with the client and advise them on how you can improve on their goals and help them achieve their objective and goals. On the consumer side, the expectation is a compelling copy offering a solution to a problem.

On top of this, you also have to manage your own expectations. If you start from a low point and aim high, you will end up stressed, burnt out and frustrated. The opposite of this statement is also something you must consider. If your expectations and goals are not challenging, you will be burnt out, stressed, and easily frustrated. To this end, you should aim to create challenging but realistic objectives.

You can do this by stating how many copies you intend to create in a day, and measuring this against your productivity. Do not give clients instant expectations (I will create your awesome copy in just a few hours). If you do this, you are likely to deliver the work in haste and thus make mistakes. On the other hand, if you offer yourself some leeway, you can exceed your expectations and impress the client. Therefore, be kind to yourself. Give a less stringent deadline but also make it challenging. The trick is to push yourself without driving off the cliff.

Adhere to the rules of ethical freelancing

To put this simply, ethical freelancing dictates the following:

\# Be truthful to yourself and your clients

\# Treat every client as you would like him or her to treat you.

\# Meet the clients expectations as well as your own expectations.

Ethical freelancing is what will set you apart from a million other copywriters. Ethical freelancing also means giving every copy the very best you have to offer. Today, value addition drives the copywriting business. While clients look for the very best people who can add some value to them and their companies, giving each copy your best guarantees your readiness to challenges and shows the client your real value. This then means you have to go out of your way to define yourself and the core values driving your copywriting business.

That is the surprise and delight strategy. It will keep you sane, happy, and productive. It will also guarantee you returning clients. Clients who give you work with a smile on their face and a guarantee of your competence to deliver outstanding work.

Conclusion

Becoming a great copywriter requires hard work and a lot of practice. Make no mistake about it. However, with what you have learned so far from reading this book, and of course should you actually apply it, you should be able to produce decent good copies that will engage and convert readers to buyers.

I will be more than happy to learn how this book has helped you in some way. If you feel you have learned something or you think it offered you some value, please take a moment to leave an honest review on Amazon. It would help many future readers who will be forever grateful to you. As I will!

To Your Success,
Adam Richards

48

DISCLAIMER AND/OR LEGAL NOTICES:

CPSIA information can be obtained at www.ICGtesting.com
Printed in the USA
LVOW10s1815020616

490980LV00026B/246/P